PODCAST MARKETING
SECRETS

INTERNET RADIO ORGANIZATION

TABLE OF CONTENTS

Introduction

Podcasts are a wonderful way to connect with your target audience and build a memorable brand. They are informative, entertaining and enlightening.

With a podcast, you can connect with a brand-new audience: people who may otherwise never and your content because they prefer audio format.

Podcasts stimulate conversations between you and your followers. Better yet, listeners will likely to become lifelong customers and promoters of your brand because they get to know you on a deeper level.

Studies show that 90% of plays and downloads come from existing podcast subscribers – people who already listen to different channels. And because they are already engaged in the community and familiar with podcasts, it'll be easy to drive traffic to not only your platform, but to different segments of your business.

In other words, a podcast will serve as a powerful springboard for your business. And the popularity and overall demand is continuing to grow every single day.

Are you ready to create a profitable podcast that will strengthen your brand and maximize exposure quickly and easily?

Let's begin!

Creating Your Podcast

There's literally no limit to what you can do with your podcast. Podcasts are as individual and unique as the people who create them. And as you work on your craft, strengthen your voice and build confidence, your podcasts will begin to attract a larger audience.

To begin, ask yourself some basic questions about your overall goals and what your target audience will likely be most interested in. This will become part of your podcast's overall theme.

Here are some common reasons for creating a podcast:

Generating business leads.

Creating brand awareness.

Cost-efficient advertising.

Increasing the size and value of your network.

Positioning yourself as an authority in your niche. Testing out new markets. Coming up with ideas for future products or services.

It's important to choose a theme or topic that aligns with your brand. This can be as broad or as narrow as you wish – just be sure to think long-term. You'll want to choose a theme that will allow you to create content regularly and over the long haul.

So, don't box yourself in with a theme or topic that is too narrow.

Another thing to keep in mind is that you should be passionate about your topic. It should be something that gets you excited to talk about so you can create fresh content regularly. It won't feel like a chore when it's time for a new episode. The more personally invested you are, the better your content will be.

One important step when coming up with a theme and topic for your podcast is to spend some time researching your niche.

Search various platforms for other podcasts in your genre or niche so you can determine what kind of content is out there, what people are most interested in and what your best approach should be.

Studying popular, established podcasts is not only a great way to evaluate the type of content that's already available to your target market, but it can help you identify areas where there is a strong demand for content that isn't easily found. It'll give you an entry point and help you come up with a unique selling point (USP) for your own channel.

You'll also want to decide on a title for your podcast and pay extra attention to the title, author, and description tags as Apple Podcasts uses these three fields for search.

Make sure your title is very clear and that your audience will understand what your focus is. A general podcast title that is too vague won't attract many subscribers, no matter how compelling the content may be.

You'll also want to make it easy for people to find your podcast, so include one or two focus keywords in the title (don't stuff the title with keywords though). Make sure they are relevant to your overall theme.

Most podcast titles are between 20 and 24 characters long, so try to keep yours short and direct. Further, you also don't need to include the word "podcast" in your title.

In addition, try to avoid ambiguous titles, or titles with numbers or symbols that could be misspelled. Your title should be easy to type into a browser and easy to remember.

Next, decide what format you want to use. Typical formats include the interview (you talk to people such as thought-leaders in your market), scripted non-fiction (serial podcasts with a single theme per season), scripted fiction (like a radio drama), the news recap (summarizing the news in your genre), and the educational podcast (scripted non-fiction that teaches your audience something).

Note: You should always spend a bit of time editing or removing any parts of the podcast that aren't particularly valuable before airing it. The length of your podcast isn't important: it's the quality that matters.

You should typically aim to publish a podcast at least once a week, both to make a regular connection with your audience and so that you're consistently broadening your outreach.

How to Build Your Audience

Now it's time to start building your audience and when it comes to podcast marketing, there are many ways of quickly generating traffic so you can build your following.

The key is to remain consistent with both your marketing efforts as well as creating new content. Every episode will go the distance in helping you maximize exposure.

Here are some of our best strategies to help you get started:

Optimize for SEO (Search Engine Optimization).

Optimizing your podcast for the search engines is one of the easiest ways to reach potential audience who may be looking for content like yours.

Focus on optimizing your title first. You'll want to incorporate relevant keywords that pertain to your podcast so your audience can easily find you.

You'll also want to optimize the description and show notes fields by including additional keywords that will help you rank in the search engines. Be sure your title and description accurately indicates what your podcast is going to be about.

Focus on High-Quality Content

You should always focus on creating the highest-quality content possible for every episode. After all, you're showcasing your talent and you want every release to "hook" a viewer and persuade them want to consume more of your content.

A quality podcast has these 3 common qualities: it's valuable to the listener, it's unique, and it captures and sustains the listener's attention.

Pay attention to podcasts in your niche. Study their format, content, style and structure. Think about how you can incorporate some of the stand-out ideas into your own podcast and improve upon the subject matter or offer a different perspective.

The best long-term strategy for promoting your podcast is by simply providing value. Nothing will come close to driving targeted traffic and converting visitors into loyal listeners than by offering exceptional content that is unique to your brand.

Encourage your viewers to participate

Ask your audience for comments and then use those comments and suggestions for future podcasts.

Try creating a podcast where you answer audience questions or create a podcast based on comment suggestions.

Aim for your audience to become subscribers

Ask your viewers to subscribe to your channel so they are noticed whenever you create a new podcast.

The ratio of subscribers to casual downloaders does matter: podcast platforms consider your podcast to be more valuable when you have a lot of subscribers. And that means your podcast will move up in the ratings.

Create a Dedicated Landing Page

By giving your podcast a dedicated landing page you're able to curate all your content in one place while encouraging visitors to subscribe to your podcast.

It's simply easier to market your podcast if you can direct all your traf c to one spot. You can use a resource like WordPress to create a blog dedicated to your podcast where you can turn each episode into its own blog post.

If creating a traditional landing page rather than a blog, make sure you use a clear and direct "call to action" asking viewers to subscribe to your podcast. Use blog content, social media announcements and newsletters to link back to this landing page.

Your goal is to spread the word quickly and direct potential subscribers to your podcasts from as many platforms as possible.

You can use a service like

https://www.ConvertKit.com to

create a landing page. Check out this

article for details:

https://convertkit.com/podcasting-landing-page

Coordinate Your Marketing Strategies

A podcast is one way of engaging your audience, but it's also a platform in which to promote your other channels (and vice versa). You need a coordinated effort across the board to maximize your results.

For example, you could run a social media contest where the winner is interviewed on your podcast, or take some of the topics presented in a podcast to expand on the content via a series of blog posts or exclusive listener-only emails.

The more coordinated you are, the easier it will be to create a system that funnels traffic throughout your business.

Create a Landing Page

Naturally, your goal is to make it as easy as possible for your audience to d you. A well-crafted landing site can help you direct potential listeners to your podcast while simultaneously building your newsletter or mailing list.

Regardless whether you're integrating your podcast into a larger content strategy that includes a blog, social media, or perhaps a website, you'll want to create a stand-out landing page that captures attention and converts a visitor into a listener.

This is often called the "home page" for your podcast – the place you'll direct your traffic so they can learn more about you and your show.

All well-designed landing pages typically includes many of the following components:

A keyword-centric description of your show and who should listen to it. You'll want to be as clear as possible with your description while including relevant keywords that can help your landing page rank in the search engines.

Multiple subscribe links, one for each major listening directory. Your social media contact information so new listeners can follow you on other platforms.

A List of your recent episodes. A way to collect email addresses for your newsletter.

This may sound intimidating, but it's not once you break it down and take it one step at a time.

Let's take a closer look:

Title and Description:

People landing on your landing page need to know why they're there and what's in it for them. This means you'll need a compelling title and an attention-grabbing description that paints a clear picture as to what your podcast is all about.

The title of your landing page can be the title of the podcast, or a catchy phrase or tagline you use in conjunction with your show. For the description, you need to answer the two main questions a viewer will have – "What is this?" and "Is This for me?"

These things may seem obvious to you but look at it from a new visitor's point. They don't know you, or know what your podcast is about, or what type of listener it's meant for. This is your chance to tell them that in a few lines.

Remember that attention spans – especially online – are very short. You may only have a matter of seconds to "hook" a visitor and get them interested in your podcast. Keep in mind that your goal is to have them subscribe to that podcast.

Make the title and initial description compelling, interesting and short enough so a visitor can glance at it and get a good idea what your podcast is about and why they want to subscribe to it.

Another thing to do is create a podcast trailer. This is normally an audio podcast with a description of your podcast set to either the opening or closing music in your podcast.

This will take some thought and a bit of work, but you can create a great title in the end.

Multiple Subscriber Links:

Apple Podcasts may be king, but it's not the only rodeo in town. You should give your listeners the option of finding your podcast on the directory and mobile app of their choice.

You'll need to submit your podcast's RSS Feed Link (which is generated by your podcast hosting provider) to each of the directories you choose.

This will take you some time, because your aim is to be on as many of those directories as possible. But with that done, the podcast will automatically update whenever you post a new episode.

The top directories are Apple Podcasts, Google, and Spotify. There are mobile apps, desktop only sites, and combinations of all the above. It may take a few hours to get everything set up, but the results will be worth it.

Once your show is approved by those directories, it's time to set up your landing page. You could use plain text links, but that's a bit amateurish.

Why not jazz it up a bit and use a button for each directory?

There's a great little plug-in from SecondLine Themes called Podcast Subscribe Buttons that makes this easy.

Once you have your subscribe buttons set up, it's time to look at the next step.

Displaying Recent Episodes:

It is important to have your previous episodes available on your page. Most distribution channels offer the opportunity to have all of the episodes together in a simple menu.

Most of the menus will show your logo, link your social media, and all of the previous episodes.

Social Media Sharing Buttons

The point of these social media sharing and connecting buttons is to have your subscribers follow you over to your social media sites and connect with you there as well.

Be sure you have a pinned post on each site asking your followers to subscribe to your podcast by visiting your landing page.

Collecting Email Addresses for Your Newsletter:

Email marketing has consistently been the highest engaging way to communicate with your followers. If you're not producing a newsletter, you should start as soon as you possibly can.

This is one of the easiest ways to advertise and connect with your followers in a meaningful way. You don't have to publish a frequent newsletter – once a month or so is fine. So long as you're communicating, your followers will remember you.

Use an email service provider like MailChimp, Drip, or Active Campaign. They'll help you collect email addresses and send messages to your subscribers whenever you have a new episode available, or have anything new to share with them.

Podcast Marketing Strategies

When it comes to launching a successful podcast, the key is to learn as much as you can about your audience so you can create content that resonates with them.

You want to not only keep a pulse on your market in terms of competing podcasts and the type of content they offer, but you should always make an effort to interact with your listeners so you can discover what they are most interested in.

Because above all else, your marketing begins long before you actively advertise your content: it starts by creating the best, most engaging content possible based on what your market is looking for. It won't matter how many marketing dollars you invest in promoting your podcast if you aren't delivering highly engaging content that connects with your target audience.

Creating an audience persona document that gives you a snapshot of your average listener will be something incredibly valuable for your podcast. You can refer to that while creating both your podcast content and your marketing campaigns. Knowing your audience is a critical component in creating a stand-out podcast that will attract listeners, so don't overlook this important step.

In addition, you want to always know your metrics when promoting your podcast so that you know exactly what works and what doesn't. Don't be afraid to try new things and always record your results. Test several methods at once, but also split-test different elements of your podcast and see what gives you the most traction.

One thing you can do is use tracking codes within your marketing campaigns, so you can see which method or source is generating the most traffic as well as providing the highest conversions.

These codes made using a service like Google Analytics URL Builder, send a source code along with the link, and tells you exactly where that specific customer came from.

Are you ready to start promoting your podcast? Here are a few strategies that will help you quickly launch, while giving you the best chance at building a loyal following of avid listeners.

Build Your Backlist

Try to offer 2-4 episodes on your launch day. The more content that is readily available, the easier it will be to encourage listeners to subscribe to your channel because the longer they'll stick around.

Online business coach Pat Flynn has this to say about it: "I actually received negative reviews from people who had listened to the first episode and were upset that there was only one."

So, keep in mind that the more episodes you have available the more invested your listeners will become. They'll better understand your style and what you are bringing to the table. And hopefully, they'll become addicted. ;)

So, one episode won't cut it. Spend some time creating a few podcasts before you sink any marketing dollars into your business.

You don't have to create a ton of content – after all, you'll want to base future podcasts on what is gaining the most traction and you won't know that before launch, but try to offer enough content to give listeners a reason to stick around.

Take Advantage of Aggregators

Send your podcast to different podcast aggregators and directories. A podcast aggregator, also called a podcatcher, is the app that plays podcasts.

The most well-known podcatcher is Apple Play, which is the default podcast app that comes with iOS.

However, there are plenty of others, including Spotify, Google Play, TuneIn, iHeartRadio, and SoundCloud, just to name a few

Create accounts with as many of these as you can, and submit your RSS feed so that your new episodes will be uploaded to each one.

This will also get your podcast before a larger audience as they scroll through their preferred app in the search for new podcasts.

Ask Listeners to Subscribe

Remind your listeners to subscribe, share, comment, and leave reviews. This goes back to focusing on creating high-quality content because you want every episode to be shareworthy.

At the beginning and end of each podcast, ask your audience to subscribe to your feed, share your podcast, comment and leave reviews of the podcast. Don't be afraid to ask!

Use Strategic Timing

Release your podcasts at strategic times. This can mean time of day, but also day of the week or month.

To do this, take advantage of podcast analytics to gure out the best times to publish according to your audience. Pay attention to when they tune in and look at where they're from, what device they're using, and what platform they're on.

Internet Radio Organization

If you're just starting out, look at podcasts similar to yours and see when they publish as well. If you notice a trend, consider following it.

Leverage Older Content

Leverage your older episodes. This is a great way to hook new subscribers. If you mention a topic you've covered in a previous episode, add a quick aside with the episode number so they can easily nd that content.

Remember to include a link in the show notes to make it even easier for your followers to nd.

Word of Mouth

Network with word-of-mouth recommendations. Word-of-mouth advertising is one of the most effective strategies out there.

Your rst step is to nd the right places to spread your message. Your audience will congregate in various platforms, ant it's your job to nd out where those places are and make sure you're there as well.

Do some research. Find out about conferences, meet-ups, and local events in your area that pertain to your podcast.

Talk to the event's attendees and speakers. Don't be afraid to mention you've got a podcast related to the topic and that's why you're there.

Look for Networking Opportunities

Network with other podcasters. The best way to stay on top of new ideas, trends and podcast techniques is to join a community of fellow podcasters.

Experienced creators are often willing to provide tips and if your content aligns with their marketing goals, you may even discover cross-promotion and other networking opportunities!

This gets both of you some extra exposure and bene ts everyone involved. Start with shows whose audiences are about the same size as yours; they're most likely to respond.

Be a Podcast Guest

Be a guest/invite a guest. Guest-starring on another podcast is a great way to introduce your content to a similar audience. And hosting interesting guests on your own podcast creates a better show for your audience.

Just make sure you ask fresh questions. Don't re-use interview questions!

Try the following resources to locate podcast creators who might be willing to guest-star on your show (or have you on theirs):

- Reddit has a group just for podcast creators who are looking for guests: r/PodcasterGuestExchange.

- Radio Guest List puts out a newsletter on Mondays and Wednesdays.

- Facebook groups like Podcast Movement or Podcaster's Support Group offer the chance to swap guest spots with other podcasters

Contribute Value Outside of the Podcast Community

Contribute value to online communities. Search platforms like Facebook, Instagram, LinkedIn, Reddit, Twitter, and Clubhouse for threads and forums relating to the topic of your podcast.

Internet Radio Organization

Search for relevant groups that have good engagement with their followers and start adding value through discussion and posting high-quality, informative information. Then, link to your podcast or landing page.

However, remember to focus on engaging with the community. Don't be a drive-by poster. Instead, focus on being part of the conversation rather than simply promoting your podcast.

Convert Your Podcast into a YouTube Video

Convert your podcast into a YouTube video to maximize exposure. A lot of people watch replays on YouTube rather than subscribe to a traditional podcast platform, so you'll want to connect with that audience as well.

The easiest way is to convert the MP3 audio le into an MP4 le. Include an image that will appear throughout the podcast and then upload.

Also, be sure to include show notes and links to your website and social channels in the description.

Customize Social Media Posts

Customize your social media posts based on each individual platform. With social media, one-size doesn't fit all. What works on Facebook

won't necessarily work on Twitter, for example. You need to switch things up when you switch social media platforms.

Study each platform to see what sorts of posts are popular, then tailor your posts to each one accordingly.

Add value on social media. Just like with online communities, you need to add to the conversations on social media instead of just peppering the audience with ad after ad. Instead, start a discussion about your topic, asking what they know or think about it. Put the focus on them instead of you.

Seize the Power of Giveaways

Launch giveaways on social media. You don't have to give away too much, but it should be something that relates to your brand.

Tip: Let your followers "earn" entries by following and sharing your podcast on social media.

Conclusion

Ultimately, a podcast is a fantastic way to grow your audience, solidify your brand, research your market and position yourself as a thought leader in your niche.

Focus on creating high-quality content that is not only relevant, but is unique in some way. While it's a smart strategy to base your content's overall theme on what has already proven to be successful, you never want to copy someone else's platform.

Find your own voice. That is what will separate you from others and help you connect with an audience that will come back for more content again and again.

Keep things simple. You'll likely expand eventually, but when just starting out, your time should be spent creating engaging content instead of spreading out too wide or trying too many things at once. Make sure your podcast has a strong and clear theme that will make sense to your audience. Don't try to cover too many topics at once unless that is part of your overall theme.

Instead, choose a handful of current topics that will resonate with your audience and focus on delivering the most engaging content possible.

Don't procrastinate! Just choose a topic, decide on your theme and create your first podcast. And keep in mind that you'll need to be consistent and reasonable with your goals. Many hosts create podcasts for five to six months before they see a major increase in the number of listeners.

That means you're likely going to be producing podcasts with little response for a while before you begin to see results.

Promoting a podcast takes time, and growth depends on consistently producing engaging and valuable content. It's well worth the effort if you want committed followers.

Keep in mind that over 42 million Americans listen to podcasts every week and the average listener goes through five shows during this time.

These are the people you want as your audience. They're regularly consuming content and always looking for relevant podcasts.

You've got this!

INTERNET RADIO ORGANIZATION

Internet Radio Organization is a one stop shop for all your podcasts needs! Here at IRO, we produce, record, edit, perform search engine optimization for each podcast, develop your cover art, and launch your podcasts so they can be directly viewed by your customers on sites like Spotify, Stitcher and ITunes.

Our process can all be done remotely via telephone, Zoom, or email. You inform us on the current industry in which your business resides, and our qualified professional will reach out to you after researching important and relevant trending topics in your industry. You will decide what topics that you like and IRO will cover one topic per week. We will then find a creative way to spin that topic and deliver it to your customers!

Our CEO, Jowanna Lewis, is a master of the art. Lewis has provided recording and event services in the music industry, written and produced podcasts for top tier businesses and created a music video awards show in the heart of Los Angeles! She is a "Jill of all trades", so rest a sure your business is in good hands!

Schedule a consultation or join us for a weekend Podcasting workshop.

Visit us online at

www.internetradioorganization.com